I Can Be An
AIRLINE PILOT

David Miller & Wilfred Hardy

DERRYDALE BOOKS
New York/Avenel, New Jersey

CONTENTS

A SALAMANDER BOOK

First published by Salamander Books Ltd.,
129-137 York Way, London N7 9LG,
United Kingdom.

© Salamander Books Ltd., 1992

ISBN 0-517-06990-3

This 1992 edition published by Derrydale Books,
distributed by Outlet Book Company, Inc.,
40 Engelhard Avenue, Avenel, New Jersey 07001.

This book may not be sold outside the United
States of America or Canada.

Printed and bound in Belgium.

8 7 6 5 4 3 2 1

CREDITS

Artwork by: Wilfred Hardy
Written by: David Miller
Edited by: Jilly Glassborow
Typeset by: Bloomsbury Graphics, London
Color separation by: P & W Graphics,
Pte. Ltd., Singapore
Printed by: Proost International Book Production,
Turnhout, Belgium

INTRODUCTION

To be an airline pilot is to have one of the
most exciting "action" jobs open to men and women
today. Every year there are more airliners in the sky,
flying more people – on business and on holiday –
to ever-more distant places. Airline pilots
make it all possible, and this colorful book
tells you exactly how they do it. So, if you've ever
wanted to know how pilots are taught to fly, how they
take off and land, and how they control their
airliners in the sky, read on. Perhaps
you will join them one day!

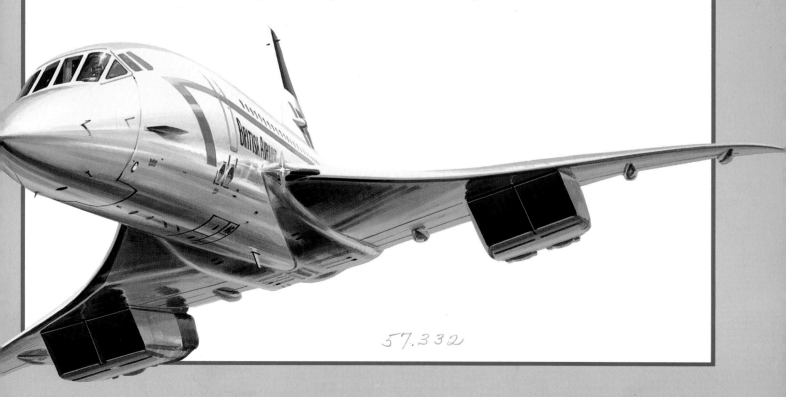

57.332

LEARNING TO FLY

The first and most exciting step for anyone who wants to be a pilot is to go along to the local flying school and register for lessons.

The instructor starts by explaining how the airplane works and flies, but soon moves on to the most thrilling part — actually flying the airplane. Lessons then continue with learning the basic maneuvers, such as taking off, climbing, turning, descending and landing.

The First Solo
For the first 18 or so lessons, the instructor sits beside the student teaching him or her all about flying. Then, one important day, the instructor says it is time to "go solo." This is a flight that no pilot ever forgets, for it means having to fly alone for the very first time, without the guidance of an instructor. After this, the student moves on to cross-country flying and advanced maneuvers. Finally, he or she graduates with a Private Pilot's Licence (PPL).

Advanced Training
All students start by learning to fly single-engined airplanes. Having got their PPL, future airline pilots must then train in twin-engined airplanes, learning how to navigate and fly using the instruments.

Everyone who wants to learn to fly starts on a small, single-engined, twin-seater trainer, like this Swedish Saab Supporter. The student is taught by an experienced and highly qualified flying instructor.

Below: This future airline pilot has graduated from a single-engined trainer to a twin-engined airplane. Here she is seen taking off on a navigation exercise, an instructor at her side.

Fire! Fire! Engine fires are impossible to practice in a real airplane but, as shown in the main picture, they are easy to recreate in a simulator.

PRACTICE IN SAFETY

Airline pilots, even after they are fully qualified, continue to be trained. They learn how to fly new airplanes and also practice what to do in an emergency. Of course, they *could* do this by flying real airliners, but that would be very expensive. It would also be very dangerous to practice emergencies such as fires or explosions during an actual flight.

Just Like the Real Thing

Instead, pilots are trained in a special machine called a simulator which acts like, or "simulates," an airliner in flight without actually leaving the ground.

From the outside a simulator looks like a huge box on stilts. The stilts, or legs, tilt

Above: From outside, a simulator looks like a moon-walker. Inside, it is so realistic that pilots think they are in a real airplane.

the box in all directions to give the sensation of climbing, descending or turning. Inside, the simulator is an exact copy of a cockpit. The pilots look through the cockpit windows at video displays which give a realistic view. In fact, pilots find simulators so lifelike that they forget they are not inside a real airplane.

Computer Control

The machine is governed by computers which create the video pictures, control the instruments and make the simulator respond to the pilot's instructions. And in overall control of each training session is an instructor who decides what problems the computer is to give the flight crew.

THE FLIGHT DECK

To us, the cockpit, or flight deck, of an airliner seems a confusing mass of dials, switches, levers and buttons. But, for pilots, it is very logical.

The captain always sits in the left hand seat, with the first officer on the right. Some older airliners also have a third flight crew member – the flight engineer – but most modern airliners are built for a crew of two.

Information and Control

In front of each pilot is a panel of instruments and displays. These tell the pilot what the airplane is doing – its direction, speed, height and so forth. In the center of the main panel is the engine display. This gives both pilots information such as engine speeds, temperatures, and fuel flow. It also includes the warning lights.

Between the seats is the central "console" (panel), which carries the engine "throttle" levers – one lever for each engine. These controls enable the pilot to alter the engine speed. The radio controls are on this console too, and are used for talking to control stations on the ground.

Essential flight instruments show the heading (direction), speed and altitude of the airplane.

The captain has two screens: one for flight information, the other for navigation.

The control column is pushed or pulled to control the "elevators" on the horizontal stabilizer (tail). Turning the handles operates the "ailerons" on the wings. (See "Controlling the Airliner.")

The foot pedals are used to control the rudder in the air and the wheel brakes on the ground.

Above: Unlike "old-fashioned" flight decks that have a mass of dials and buttons, the flight deck of a modern Boeing 747-400 is much simpler. Almost all the dials have been replaced by three TV-type screens called cathode-ray tubes.

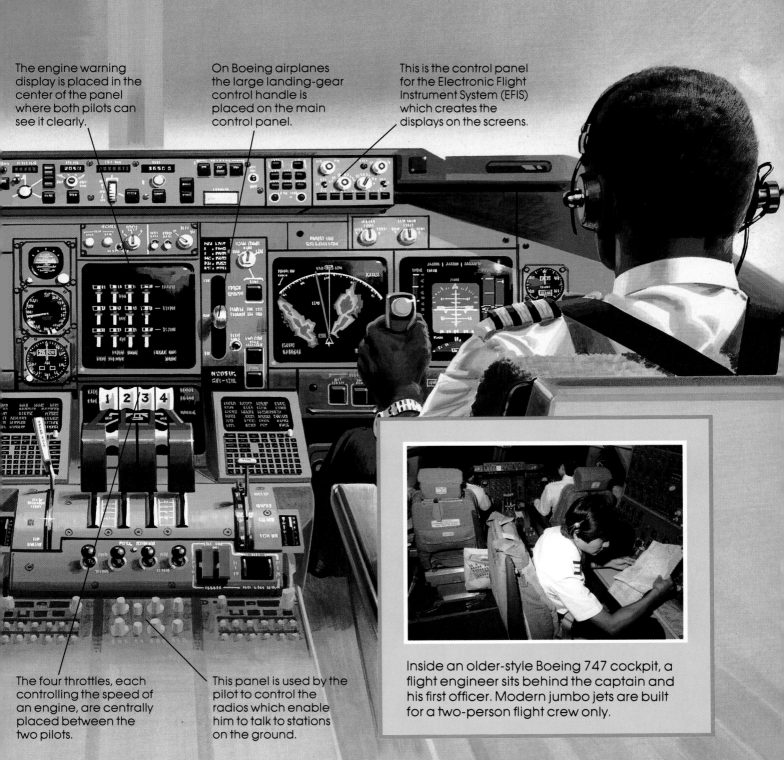

The engine warning display is placed in the center of the panel where both pilots can see it clearly.

On Boeing airplanes the large landing-gear control handle is placed on the main control panel.

This is the control panel for the Electronic Flight Instrument System (EFIS) which creates the displays on the screens.

The four throttles, each controlling the speed of an engine, are centrally placed between the two pilots.

This panel is used by the pilot to control the radios which enable him to talk to stations on the ground.

Inside an older-style Boeing 747 cockpit, a flight engineer sits behind the captain and his first officer. Modern jumbo jets are built for a two-person flight crew only.

PREPARING FOR FLIGHT

Before taking off on any flight, an airline captain and his or her first officer must report to the briefing center. Here they get data from a computer about their flight – the number of passengers, the performance of their airplane, weather conditions and possible routes. The captain then decides which route to follow, and the first officer calculates the amount of fuel that will be needed for the flight.

Fit to Fly
At the same time, out on the ramps, ground engineers carefully check the airplane to see that everything is in perfect working order – that it is "fit to fly." The airliner is then cleaned, inside and out.

Next, a tanker truck fills the craft's tanks with the required amount of fuel.

The Final Preparations
After their briefing, both the captain and the first officer join their airliner and enter the cockpit. Here they carry out various cockpit checks to make absolutely sure that everything is working.

The cabin crew, having had their own briefing, check that the seats and safety equipment are prepared, and that all the food and drinks are loaded. Finally, the captain decides that the airplane is ready and the passengers are boarded.

As the captain boards his Fokker 50 airliner, the first officer has a final check with the chief ground engineer.

During the briefing, the captain receives flight information from computers. The captain must then plan the flight, knowing that the responsibility for the airplane is his or hers alone.

TAKE-OFF

When everything is ready and the passengers are seated, the pilot taxies the airliner, under orders from the ground movement controller, to a "holding" point near the end of the runway. Finally, "clearance" is given by air traffic control and the pilot moves the airliner on to the runway, ready for take-off.

During take-off there are three "critical" speeds, which are worked out beforehand. At the first speed the captain must decide whether or not to go on. If he, or she, decides to abandon take-off (perhaps because an engine is faulty) he slows down using the brakes and "thrust reversers" (which literally reverse the direction of thrust in the engines) to stop the airliner before it reaches the end of the runway.

If, as is far more likely, the captain decides to go on with the take-off, the airliner next reaches the take-off speed (speed two), at which time the captain pulls the control column back and the airliner soars into the air. The first officer then retracts (pulls in) the wheels, or landing gear, and the captain takes the airliner at the best speed (speed three) and angle for the climb, up into the sky.

Keeping the Noise Down

At the start of the climb the captain pays special attention to the noise of the engines, so that people living nearby are disturbed as little as possible. To keep the noise down the captain may climb steeply to 1000ft while still within the airport limits and then reduce power for a shallower climb, so making less noise. Only when the airliner has reached cruising height can the captain relax.

HOW A JET ENGINE WORKS

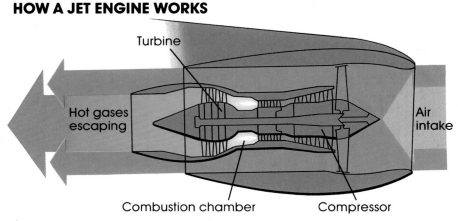

Turbine

Hot gases escaping

Combustion chamber

Compressor

Air intake

Air enters the engine via the intakes. It is speeded up by the compressor and forced into the combustion chambers. Here it is mixed with fuel and ignited (burnt). The resulting hot gases rush backward, driving the turbine as they go, and thrusting the airplane forward. The turbine, in turn, drives the compressor.

CONTROLLING THE AIRLINER

Inside the cockpit, each pilot has a control column with a handle on top. The pilot turns this – rather like the steering wheel in a car – to make the airliner turn left or right. But, unlike a car, an airliner can also move up and down. This movement is controlled by pushing the control column forward to make the airplane descend or pulling it back to make it climb.

Both the pilots rest their feet on pedals which, in the air, are used to control the "rudder" – a control surface on the tail. On the ground the pedals are used to control the brakes. Other controls include one set of throttles, which alter the speed of the engines, and one set of flap levers, which control the wing flaps. Both of these are placed between the two pilots so that either can control them.

Rods and Levers

When the pilots move their controls the signals are passed either to control surfaces on the wings and tail or to the engines. In small airplanes the connections are made by rods, levers

The two **pilots** sit on the flight deck, with the captain on the left.

The **engines** on this Airbus A330 are mounted on pylons (supports) under the wings. They provide the thrust to drive the airplane forward.

The many movable control surfaces on this Airbus A330 are clearly outlined. Using the "fly-by-wire" system, the pilots control the movement of these surfaces from the cockpit.

Winglets are used to increase the lift and improve the performance of the wing.

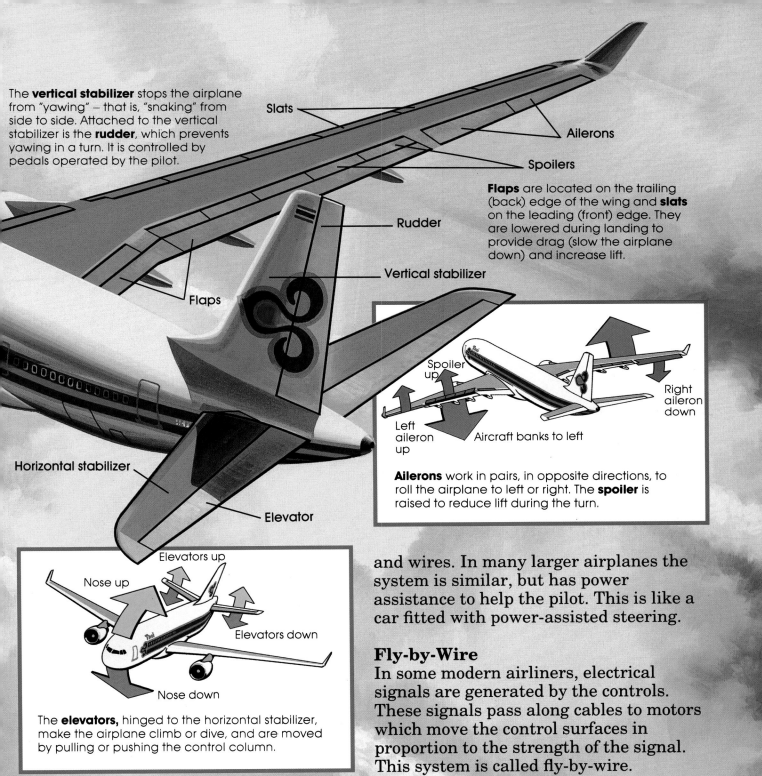

The **vertical stabilizer** stops the airplane from "yawing" – that is, "snaking" from side to side. Attached to the vertical stabilizer is the **rudder**, which prevents yawing in a turn. It is controlled by pedals operated by the pilot.

Slats

Ailerons

Spoilers

Rudder

Flaps are located on the trailing (back) edge of the wing and **slats** on the leading (front) edge. They are lowered during landing to provide drag (slow the airplane down) and increase lift.

Flaps

Vertical stabilizer

Spoiler up

Right aileron down

Left aileron up

Aircraft banks to left

Ailerons work in pairs, in opposite directions, to roll the airplane to left or right. The **spoiler** is raised to reduce lift during the turn.

Horizontal stabilizer

Elevator

Elevators up

Nose up

Elevators down

Nose down

The **elevators,** hinged to the horizontal stabilizer, make the airplane climb or dive, and are moved by pulling or pushing the control column.

and wires. In many larger airplanes the system is similar, but has power assistance to help the pilot. This is like a car fitted with power-assisted steering.

Fly-by-Wire
In some modern airliners, electrical signals are generated by the controls. These signals pass along cables to motors which move the control surfaces in proportion to the strength of the signal. This system is called fly-by-wire.

KEEPING IN TOUCH

Most airliners are fitted with a small radar that tells the pilot what the weather is like ahead.

Radio beacons are located over most countries in the world. They enable airplanes to work out their position.

In flight, the captain uses the radio to keep in touch with controllers on the ground. Over short distances VHF (very high frequency) radio is used, which is like the FM broadcasts we have at home. But for longer ranges, such as when the airplane is over the sea, HF (high frequency) is used, because such signals can travel much greater distances. Satellites also give information on the airplane's position.

At an air traffic control center, a controller sits in front of a radar screen. He uses the information he receives to control the movements of all airplanes in his sector.

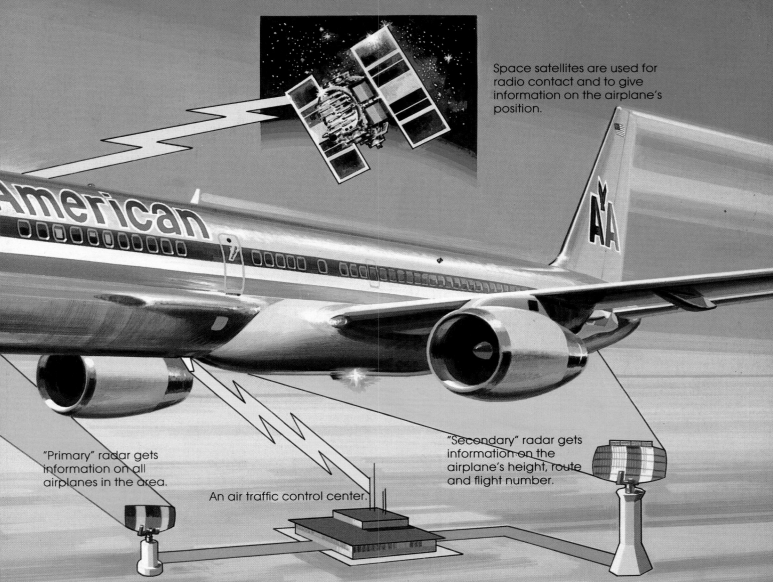

Space satellites are used for radio contact and to give information on the airplane's position.

"Primary" radar gets information on all airplanes in the area.

"Secondary" radar gets information on the airplane's height, route and flight number.

An air traffic control center.

In air traffic control centers on the ground, controllers use two types of radar to follow airplane movements. One type is used to give a picture of all airplanes in the area. The other radar sends out signals to each airplane. The airplane automatically replies, using a device called a "transponder." The transponder gives the airplane's identity, and also gives its height and route.

How Pilots Navigate

One way pilots work out where they are is by using a navigation system based on radio beacons. When an airplane signals a beacon, the beacon sends an automatic reply. A device on the airplane times how long the reply takes to arrive and works out how far the airplane is from the beacon. By getting distances from several beacons pilots can plot where they are.

COMING IN TO LAND

For any airline pilot, landing is one of the most difficult jobs he or she has to do. Every landing needs great skill and concentration, and each one is a new challenge.

Landings start with the air traffic controller telling the captain which runway to land on and the direction of approach. This will almost always be into the wind to give as short a landing run as possible. The captain turns on to the approach and points the airplane's nose down by gently easing the control column forward. Next the throttles are slowly closed in order to lose speed.

Approaching the Runway

The captain then lowers the wing flaps (as shown in the diagram on the right) which gives extra lift at slow speeds, and raises the spoilers to increase drag. Finally, the landing gear is lowered. When the airliner is just a few feet above the runway the captain pulls the nose up and the wheels gently touch the ground. Touchdown is usually at speeds of between 120 and 160mph.

Spoilers raised

Flaps lowered

SUPERSONIC PILOT

For today's airline pilots, the most exciting airplane they can fly is the supersonic Concorde. Not only is it the fastest airliner in the skies, traveling at twice the speed of sound (supersonic means faster than sound), it is also considered by many people to be the most beautiful airplane in the world.

Faster Than a Bullet

Everyone who has ever flown in Concorde comments on how exciting it is. The four Olympus turbojet engines make it as powerful as a jet fighter, enabling the airplane to climb at almost a mile per minute to reach a maximum height of 60,000ft. It normally flies at 51,000ft where it cruises at 1300mph – faster than a rifle bullet. The skies at such heights are empty because no other airliners fly above 40,000ft. It is so high that pilots and passengers can see the curve of the Earth's surface.

Right: For airline pilots Concorde is the most exciting airliner they can fly. Every line of this beautiful airplane shows that it is designed for speed, cruising at twice the speed of sound (1300mph).

Right: Pilots practice flying at supersonic speeds in the cockpit of a Concorde simulator. Everything in the cockpit is just like the real thing but the view through the window is created by a large computer.

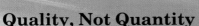

Quality, Not Quantity

There are just 14 Concordes in service today, in comparison to 1000 or so 747s. They fly only three routes, two of which are run by British Airways – between London and New York, and London and Washington. The third service is run by Air France between Paris and New York. The flights are famous for their comfort, reliability and, above all, speed.

When Time Is Money

Unfortunately, Concorde is an extremely expensive airliner to operate, and tickets are very costly. Therefore, most of the people who travel by Concorde, such as business executives, film and TV stars, and politicians, do so because time is more important than money. They fly supersonic so they spend as little time as possible in traveling.

Above: Helicopter pilots lead exciting lives, flying at low level, in all weathers and using only small landing pads. This French Puma helicopter has just taken off from an oil-rig.

HELICOPTER PILOT

Airline pilots may also fly helicopters, which are very exciting airplanes. Unlike most airplanes they can go straight up or down, hover, and travel backward or sideways, as well as forward. Also, they do not need runways like normal airplanes, but can land on almost any flat surface.

Slow But Agile

The fastest helicopter flies at about 180mph which is not nearly as fast as a fixed-wing airliner. But helicopters make up for this slowness by their amazing maneuverability which enables them to take passengers to places where no other transportation can go. They can land on the roof of a building in a city centre, in a clearing in the middle of the jungle or on a small platform on an oil-rig. Helicopters can also fly in bad weather and are often used for daring rescues on mountains or at sea; they have saved many people's lives.

With their ability to take off and land vertically, helicopters can carry passengers into the heart of big cities.

TOMORROW'S PILOT

What does the future hold for airlines and their pilots? One thing is certain – more and more people will want to travel by air, and tomorrow's airline pilot will be in great demand. Passengers will also want to fly farther afield for less money, so airlines will need airplanes that are inexpensive to operate and can travel non-stop over great distances.

It is far more difficult, however, to predict what sort of airplane tomorrow's pilot will be flying. Will they be subsonic, like the majority of today's airliners, or will they be supersonic like the Concorde?

Above: Tomorrow's airline pilot may be flying outside the Earth's atmosphere at four times the speed of sound.

Supersonic Airliners

Airplane manufacturers may decide to develop new supersonic airliners, flying at four times the speed of sound. These airliners would fly so high that they would almost be in orbit in space. They would carry 200 passengers to the other side of the world in between 60 and 90 minutes! But it would cost a *vast* amount of money to develop such airplanes and they would be *very* expensive to operate.

Subsonic Airlines

The alternative is to continue to develop subsonic airliners, so that they can carry more people over greater distances. Today the Boeing 747-400 can fly 400 people non-stop for 8000 miles. So perhaps, in ten years time, there will be airliners carrying 800 people non-stop for 10,000 miles. For such airliners, every place on Earth would be within non-stop flying distance!

USEFUL TERMS

Note: Words printed in capital letters have separate entries.

Ailerons Hinged plates on the outer end of the wings' TRAILING EDGE. They work in opposite directions to each other – moving upward on one wing and downward on the other – and are used to make the airplane bank (see BANKING).

Airfoil The shape of an airplane wing in cross-section. The wing is curved at the top and flat underneath. This causes the air to move faster over the top of the wing than beneath it, creating the lift that keeps the airplane in the sky.

Air traffic control A center from which airplanes in flight are controlled. Air traffic controllers use RADAR to track (follow) the airplanes. They also give instructions to the airliner captains by radio.

Automatic pilot A device that automatically flies the airplane safely on course without the aid of the pilot. The captain hands over to the automatic pilot (commonly known as "George") once the airliner is at cruising height and speed, and is on course.

Banking Making a turn in an airplane, during which one wing is raised higher than the other so that the craft "leans" into the turn.

Beacon A small unmanned radio station on the ground. It transmits a continuous radio signal which pilots use for navigation.

Briefing The meeting where the captain and the first officer are given information about the flight, such as details of weather conditions along the route, the number of passengers and the amount of freight to be carried.

Control column A device on the flight deck used by the pilots to control the airplane. It consists of a column with a handle on the end. Turning the handle turns the airplane to the right or left; pulling or pushing the column causes the airplane to climb or descend respectively.

Drag The force which tends to slow an airplane down. It is caused by resistance to the air flowing over the surface of the craft. To reduce the drag the shape of an airliner is designed to be as smooth as possible – this technique is called "streamlining."

Elevators Movable plates on the horizontal stabilizer (see TAIL) at the back of the airplane. They are hinged on to the tailplane (the fixed part of the stabilizer) and can be raised or lowered by the pilot to make the airplane climb or dive respectively.

Flaps Large movable plates mounted on the TRAILING EDGE of the wing. The pilot lowers them when coming in to land to give extra lift and to slow the airplane down.

Fuselage The main body of an airliner. It is a tubular structure that houses the crew and the passengers on the upper deck, and the cargo and passengers' baggage in the cargo hold underneath.

Holding pattern An oblong flight path flown by airliners while they are waiting to land.

Landing gear The wheels that support the airplane on the ground. There are two sets of wheels under the wings, known as the "main wheels." The third wheel at the front is known as the "nosewheel."

Leading edge The blunt, front edge of the wing.

Lift The upward force which supports the weight of an airliner in the air. It is caused by air flowing over the AIRFOILS.

Radar A stream of radio waves used to detect the position of airplanes in the sky. The waves are sent by AIR TRAFFIC CONTROL. When they hit an airplane some of the waves are bounced back and the returning signal (which is rather like an echo) is displayed as a bright spot (or "blip") on a screen.

Rudder A movable plate on the vertical stabilizer (see TAIL) at the back of the airplane. It is hinged onto the fin and can be turned to left or right to control the airplane in a turn.

Simulator A machine used for training pilots on the ground. An exact copy of a cockpit, coupled with computer-controlled displays, reproduces on the ground what would happen in a real airliner in the sky.

Slats Movable plates fitted on the LEADING EDGE of the wings. When coming in to land or flying at low speeds, the pilot lowers the slats to maintain LIFT.

Solo Meaning "alone." The first flight made by a student pilot without an instructor is called the "solo flight."

Spoilers Movable plates on the upper surface of the wings which are raised to lose, or "dump," lift on landing, so increasing the load on the wheels. They are also used as air brakes to slow the airplane down when starting the descent to a landing.

Stabilizer See TAIL.

Supersonic Faster than the speed of sound ("sonic" meaning sound and "super" meaning greater than). There are many supersonic military airplanes in service today but the only supersonic airliner is Concorde.

Tail The rear part of the airplane, consisting of the vertical stabilizer (or fin) and the horizontal stabilizer (or tailplane). The RUDDER is attached to the fin and the ELEVATORS are attached to the tailplane.

Throttle A lever, mounted on the flight deck, which controls the speed of an engine. There is one throttle for each engine.

Trailing edge The sharp rear (back) edge of the wing.

Turbofan A type of engine that combines the best features of the TURBOJET and TURBOPROP. It has oversize blades at the front of the compressor which revolve in a circular "duct."

Turbojet A type of engine in which a compressor drives air into combustion chambers. Here the air is mixed with fuel and burnt. The resulting hot gases escape at high speed through a turbine and drive the airplane forward.

Turboprop A type of engine in which a TURBOJET is used to drive a propeller. It is quieter than a turbojet and uses less fuel at lower speeds, but is not suitable for very high speeds.

WHAT TO DO, WHERE TO GO?

Now that you have read this book and know something about the life of an airline pilot, you probably want to know how you can become an airline pilot too.

The first thing to realize is that *all* airlines set very high standards for their aircrew. Anyone applying to become a pilot will be tested for physical fitness, eyesight, leadership qualities, mental alertness and motivation.

Applicants must also have the necessary school or college examination results, for example, mathematics and at least one science subject are usually required.

Where to Start

If you want to become an airline pilot, you could contact the airline of your choice and ask them to send you full details of their requirements and training scheme. Then you can work out whether you might be the type of person they are looking for and start to prepare yourself – for example, by taking the correct examinations.

Airline Requirements

Some airlines, such as British Airways and Qantas, accept young men and women with no flying experience and give them a complete training course. Others, such as United Airlines and Air New Zealand, only accept pilots who are already qualified. Most airlines also accept military pilots and retrain them to fly civil airliners.

To give you an idea of what airlines are looking for, here are the requirements of two of the world's largest airlines.

United Airlines in the United States only accepts pilots who are already qualified. They must have completed 350 hours as a captain or co-pilot on a fixed wing aircraft. They must also hold an instrument rating, possess a flight engineer certificate, and pass the medical examinations. Having been accepted for the airline, the training course then lasts six weeks.

British Airways, the largest airline in Europe, trains most of its own pilots. Applicants must be between the ages of 18 and 24; having been accepted, they are trained for 70 weeks, at the end of which they get a Commercial Pilot's Licence.

Flying Schools

If you want to learn to fly before applying to an airline, you should start by finding your nearest flying school. Look out for advertisements in your local paper or look in the telephone directory. Although most countries have no minimum age for flying with a qualified instructor, most do set a minimum age of 17 for flying solo or holding a PPL (Private Pilot's Licence).

In order to learn, most people need at least 40 hours of flying, which can be spread over as little as a month or as much as a year. You will also have to study a number of other subjects at "ground school", such as flying regulations, piloting procedures and navigation. Finally, at the end of your training, you will be tested on all areas and, if successful, will be awarded your PPL.